TOOLS FOR CAREGIVERS

- **F&P LEVEL:** B
- **WORD COUNT:** 112
- **CURRICULUM CONNECTIONS:** alphabet, spelling

Skills to Teach

- **HIGH-FREQUENCY WORDS:** for, is, you
- **CONTENT WORDS:** apple, bullfrog, car, dog, elephant, flower, grapes, house, igloo, jelly, kangaroo, know, letters, lizard, moon, nest, now, owl, pumpkin, quilt, robot, snake, tiger, umbrella, vulture, whale, X-ray, yarn, zebra
- **PUNCTUATION:** exclamation points, periods
- **WORD STUDY:** compound word (*bullfrog*); long *a*, spelled *ay* (*X-ray*); long e, spelled *y* (*jelly*); long o, spelled *ow* (*know*); oo sound, spelled oo (*igloo*, *kangaroo*, *moon*); ow sound, spelled *ou* (*house*); ow sound, spelled *ow* (*flower*, *now*, *owl*)
- **TEXT TYPE:** information report

Before Reading Activities

- Read the title and give a simple statement of the main idea.
- Have students "walk" though the book and talk about what they see in the pictures.
- Introduce new vocabulary by having students predict the first letter and locate the word in the text.
- Discuss any unfamiliar concepts that are in the text.

After Reading Activities

The Let's Review! activity in the book asks readers to spell out their name and identify what letter it starts with. Can each reader name the other letters in his or her name? What about the letters in their last names? Have the readers pair up. See if they can sound out their partner's name and then spell it out.

Tadpole Books are published by Jump!, 5357 Penn Avenue South, Minneapolis, MN 55419, www.jumplibrary.com

Copyright ©2020 Jump. International copyright reserved in all countries. No part of this book may be reproduced in any form without written permission from the publisher.

Editor: Jenna Trnka **Designer:** Anna Peterson

Photo Credits: Magdziak Marcin/Adobe Stock, cover; skodonnell/iStock, 1; Steve Debenport/iStock, 2t; Sir_Eagle, 2b; Dionisvera/Shutterstock, 3t; AlexandrMoroz/iStock, 3b; MilsiArt/Shutterstock, 4t; haru/Shutterstock, 4b; pchoui/iStock, 5t, 14b; chengyuzheng/iStock, 5b; Rafal Olechowski/Shutterstock, 6t; Joe Belanger/Shutterstock, 6b; Michel Cecconi/Shutterstock, 7t; Bradley Blackburn/Shutterstock, 7b; Amwu/Dreamstime, 8t; JRP Studio/Shutterstock, 8b; vovan/Shutterstock, 9t; BirdImages/iStock, 9b; topseller/Shutterstock, 10t; Sergey Klopotov/Dreamstime, 10b; melnikof/Shutterstock, 11t; Eric Isselee/Shutterstock, 11b, 12t; Glenn Bartlet/All Canada Photos/SuperStock, 12b; New Africa/Shutterstock, 13t; Andrea Izzotti/iStock, 13b; MaryAnne Campbell/Shutterstock, 14t; M Kunz/Shutterstock, 15t; Aaron Amat/Shutterstock, 15b; Andy Dean Photography/Shutterstock, 16.

Library of Congress Cataloging-in-Publication Data
Names: Peterson, Anna C., 1982– author. | Title: Let's learn letters / by Anna C. Peterson.
Description: Minneapolis, MN: Jump!, Inc., (2020) | Series: Fun first concepts | Audience: Ages 3–6.
Identifiers: LCCN 2019032371 (print) | LCCN 2019032372 (ebook) | ISBN 9781645273172 (hardcover) | ISBN 9781645273189 (paperback) ISBN 9781645273196 (ebook)
Subjects: LCSH: English language—Alphabet—Juvenile literature.
Classification: LCC PE1155 .P48 2020 (print) | LCC PE1155 (ebook) | DDC 421/.1—dc23
LC record available at https://lccn.loc.gov/2019032371
LC ebook record available at https://lccn.loc.gov/2019032372

FUN FIRST CONCEPTS

LET'S LEARN LETTERS

by Anna C. Peterson

TABLE OF CONTENTS

tadpole
books

LET'S LEARN LETTERS!

Bb

B is for bullfrog.

Aa

A is for apple.

Cc

C is for car.

Dd

D is for dog.

Ff

F is for flower.

Ee

E is for elephant.

Gg

G is for grapes.

Hh

H is for house.

Jj

J is for jelly.

I i

I is for igloo.

K k

K is for kangaroo.

Ll

L is for lizard.

Nn

N is for nest.

Mm

M is for moon.

Oo

O is for owl.

Pp

P is for pumpkin.

Rr

R is for robot.

Qq

Q is for quilt.

Ss

S is for snake.

Tt

T is for tiger.

Vv

V is for vulture.

Uu

U is for umbrella.

Ww

W is for whale.

Xx

X is for X-ray.

Zz

Z is for zebra.

Yy

Y is for yarn.

Now you know letters!

LET'S REVIEW!

Write out your name. What letter does it start with? What other things start with that letter?

LETTER CHART

Aa Bb Cc Dd Ee Ff
Gg Hh Ii Jj Kk Ll
Mm Nn Oo Pp Qq Rr
Ss Tt Uu Vv Ww Xx
Yy Zz